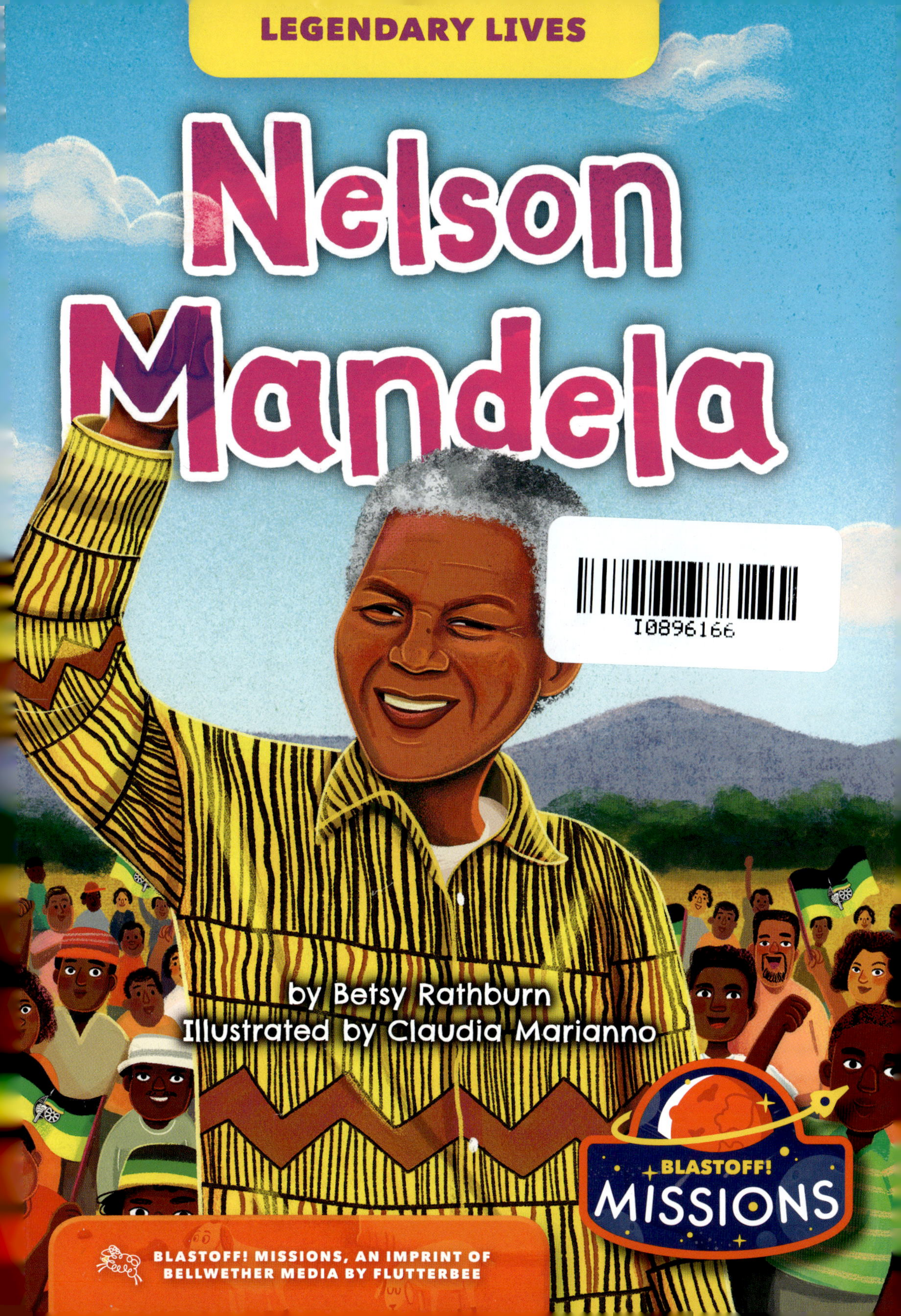
LEGENDARY LIVES
Nelson Mandela
by Betsy Rathburn
Illustrated by Claudia Marianno
BLASTOFF! MISSIONS
BLASTOFF! MISSIONS, AN IMPRINT OF BELLWETHER MEDIA BY FLUTTERBEE

Blastoff! Missions takes you on a learning adventure! Colorful illustrations and exciting narratives highlight cool facts about our world and beyond. Read the mission goals and follow the narrative to gain knowledge, build reading skills, and have fun!

Traditional Nonfiction

Narrative Nonfiction

Blastoff! Universe

MISSION GOALS

- FIND YOUR SIGHT WORDS IN THE BOOK.
- LEARN MORE ABOUT NELSON MANDELA'S LIFE.
- LEARN HOW NELSON MANDELA BECAME SOUTH AFRICA'S FIRST PRESIDENT.

This edition first published in 2026 by Bellwether Media, Inc.

For information regarding permission, write to Bellwether Media, Inc., Attention: Permissions Department, 3500 American Blvd W, Suite 150, Bloomington, MN 55431.

Library of Congress Cataloging-in-Publication Data is available at www.loc.gov or upon request from the publisher.

ISBN: 9798893048452 (hardcover)
ISBN: 9798898800192 (paperback)
ISBN: 9798893049459 (ebook)

Editor: Rebecca Sabelko Designer: Andrea Schneider

Printed in the United States of America, North Mankato, MN.

This is **Blastoff Jimmy**! He is here to help you on your mission and share fun facts along the way!

Table of Contents

A Fearless Leader

Nelson Mandela is on **trial**. He gives a speech against the **injustice** faced by Black South Africans. He says he is prepared to die for his beliefs.

I am prepared to die.

Growing Up

JIMMY SAYS

Nelson's birth name was Rolihlahla. He had to start using the name Nelson when he started school.

Nelson lives in a small village in South Africa. He is part of a **clan** of the Thembu people. His father is the clan's **chief**.

Nelson is 12. His father has passed away. Now he lives with a leader of the Thembu people.

Nelson goes to good schools.
He studies hard.

Now Nelson is in **college**. He studies law. He wants to fight the unfair laws Black South Africans face. Few can vote. Schools for Black children get little money.

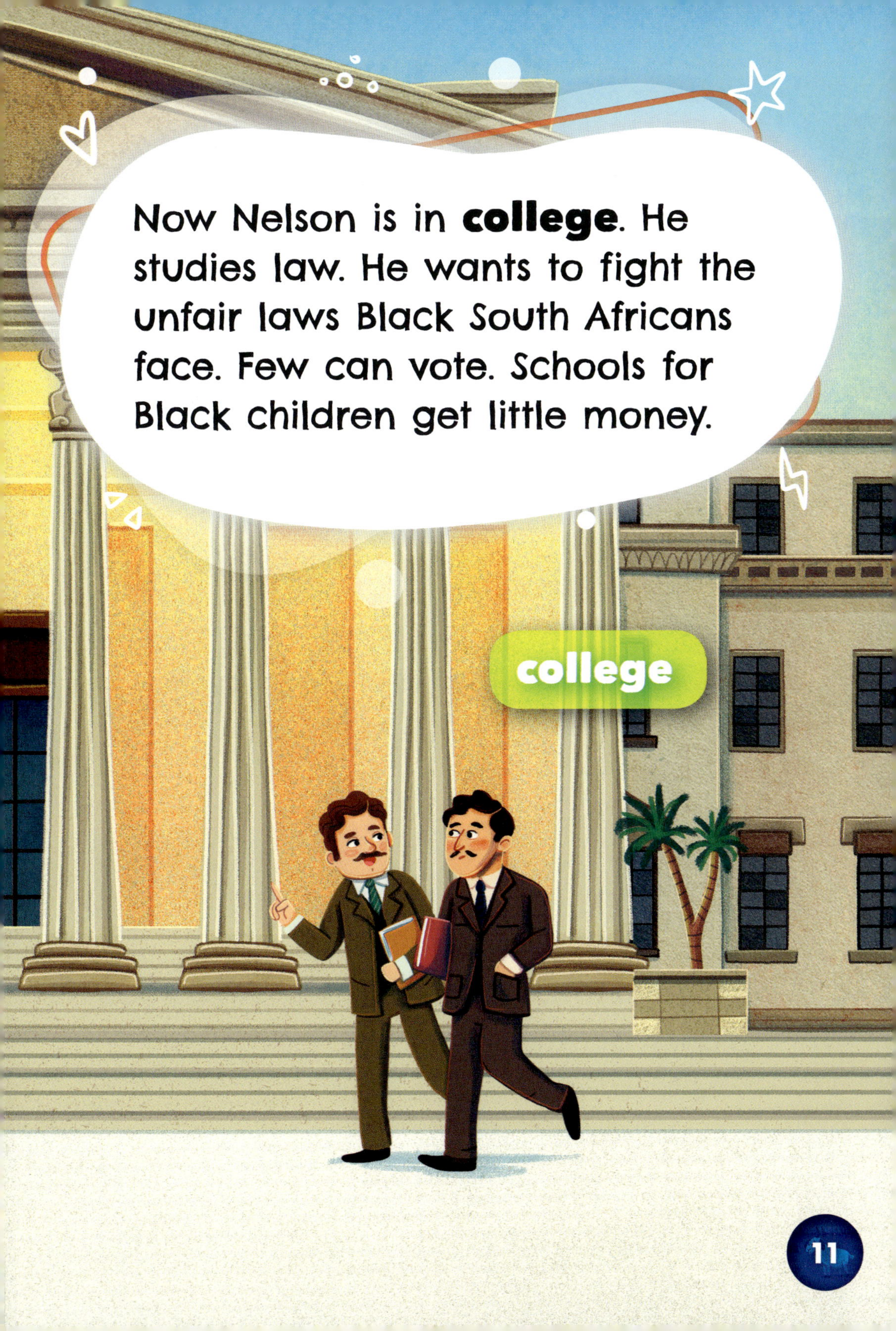

Working for Change

South Africa is under **apartheid**. Laws do not let Black people work certain jobs. They cannot vote. They cannot travel freely.

Nelson helps lead a group to fight these laws.

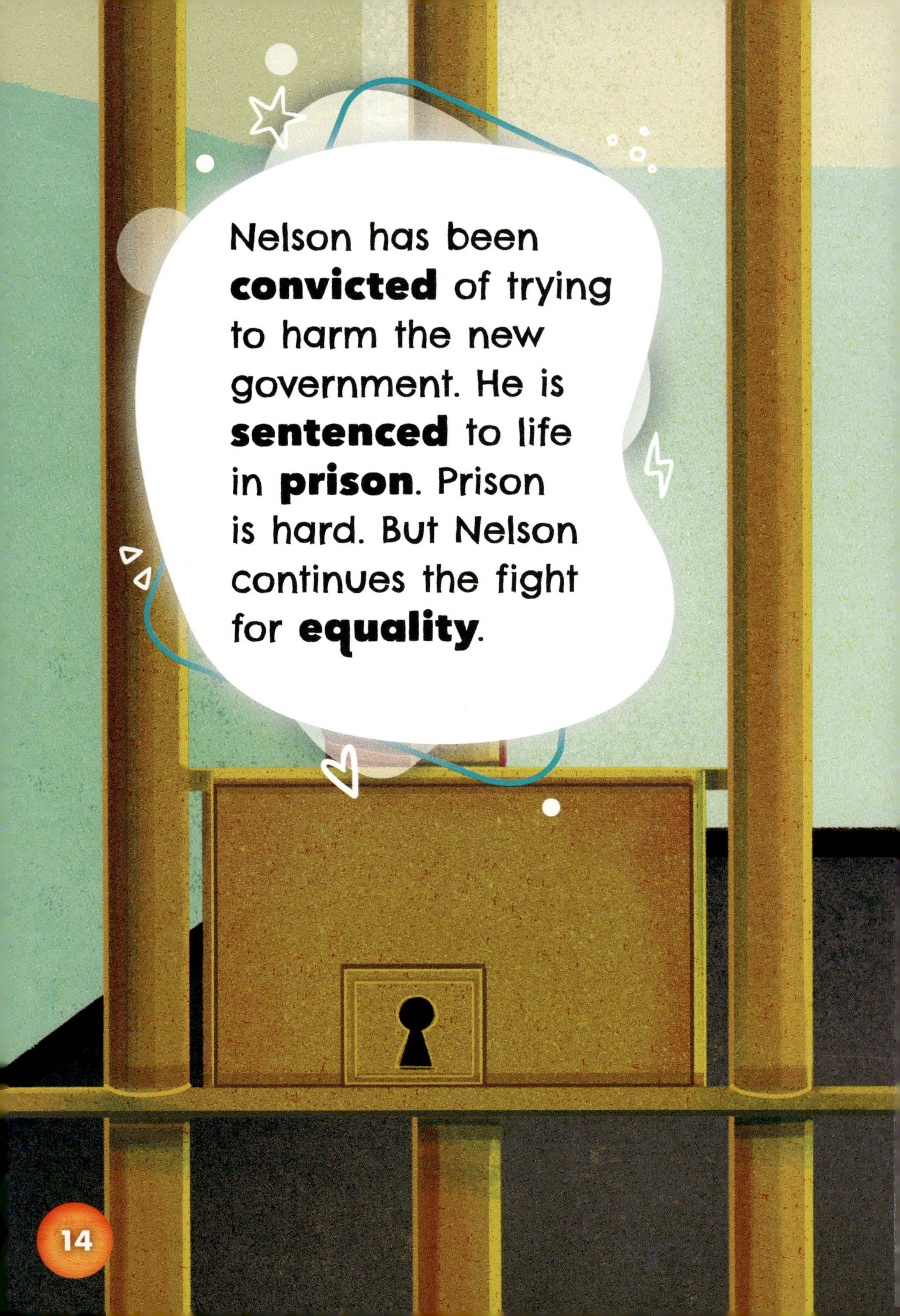

Nelson has been **convicted** of trying to harm the new government. He is **sentenced** to life in **prison**. Prison is hard. But Nelson continues the fight for **equality**.

prison

It is 1990. A new president is working to end apartheid.

He knows Nelson was treated unfairly. Nelson is freed from prison after 27 years.

IEC

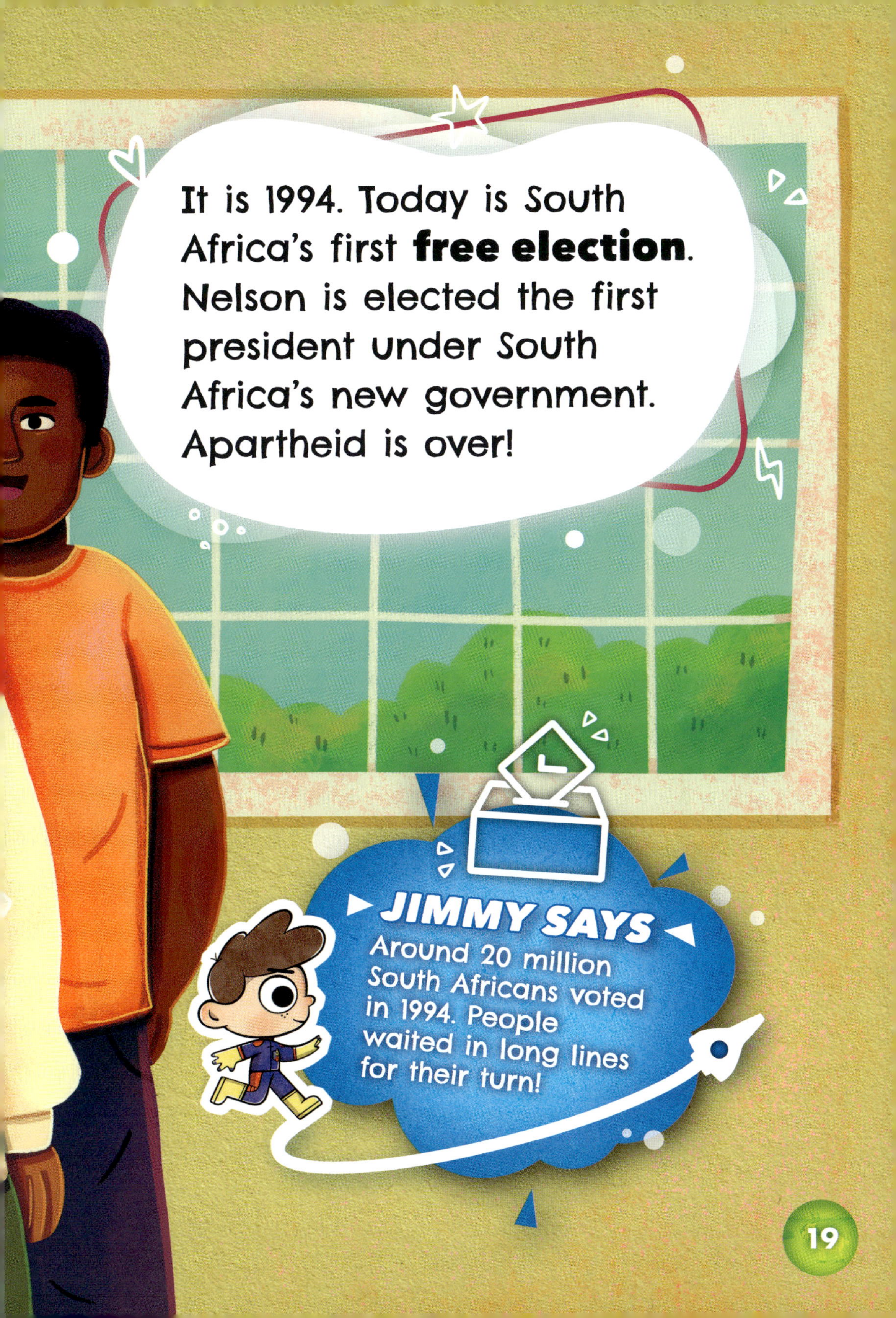

It is 1994. Today is South Africa's first **free election**. Nelson is elected the first president under South Africa's new government. Apartheid is over!

JIMMY SAYS

Around 20 million South Africans voted in 1994. People waited in long lines for their turn!

The Fight Goes On

Today, Nelson speaks to a crowd in England. He tells people to keep working toward justice. Nelson's fight against apartheid has ended. But his work **inspires** others to fight on!

Nelson Mandela Profile

Born

July 18, 1918, in
Mvezo, South Africa

Died

December 5, 2013

Accomplishments

Fought to end apartheid and became the first president of South Africa

Timeline

1925: starts school and has to use the name Nelson

1948: apartheid laws go into effect in South Africa

1964: is sentenced to life in prison

1990: is released from prison after 27 years

1994: votes for the first time and is elected South Africa's first president

Glossary

apartheid—a system of unequal treatment in South Africa based on race

chief—leader

clan—a group of people within a larger group

college—a school for higher learning

convicted—found guilty of a crime

equality—fair treatment for all groups

free election—an election in which all people can safely vote for the person of their choice

injustice—unfair treatment

inspires—gives ideas about what to do or create

prison—a place a person is kept after being found guilty of breaking a law

sentenced—made to spend time in prison for breaking a law

trial—an event to decide if a person broke a law

To Learn More

AT THE LIBRARY

Krensky, Stephen. *Nelson Mandela.* New York, N.Y.: DK Publishing, 2019.

Rathburn, Betsy. *John Lewis.* Minneapolis, Minn.: Bellwether Media, 2025.

Wilson, Wayne L. *Peaceful Protests: Voices for Civil Rights: Mahatma Gandhi, Medgar Evers, Rosa Parks, Martin Luther King Jr., Nelson Mandela.* Mount Joy, Pa.: Curious Fox Books, 2024.

ON THE WEB

FACTSURFER

Factsurfer.com gives you a safe, fun way to find more information.

1. Go to www.factsurfer.com.
2. Enter "Nelson Mandela" into the search box and click 🔍.
3. Select your book cover to see a list of related content.

BEYOND THE MISSION

> WHAT FACT FROM THE BOOK DID YOU THINK WAS THE MOST INTERESTING?

> WHAT QUESTIONS WOULD YOU ASK NELSON ABOUT HIS LIFE?

> DO YOU THINK IT WAS OKAY FOR NELSON TO BREAK LAWS? WHY OR WHY NOT?

Index